# Oh No! Another Senior Moment

## More prayers, sayings and chuckles

Inspired by Faith

Oh No! Another Senior Moment
©Product Concept Mfg., Inc.

Oh No! Another Senior Moment
ISBN 978-0-9843328-7-8

Published by Product Concept Mfg., Inc.
2175 N. Academy Circle #200, Colorado Springs, CO 80909

©2010 Product Concept Mfg., Inc.  All rights reserved.

Where quotations do not have a credit, the author is unknown.

# The older you get,
## it's funny how...

...what you thought you heard is so
much more entertaining than what
was actually said.

...you come to realize that some
mistakes are way too much fun to
make only once in life.

... your knees buckle,
but your belt won't.

. . . . . . . . . . . . . . . .

# "Seen it all...
## done it all...
### and can't remember
### any of it!"

. . . . . . . . . . . . . . . .

# Oh No! Another Senior Moment

...an answer to
"How do you feel?"
can take up the better part
of an afternoon.

...your back goes out
more than you do.

... everything is over by the
time you find your glasses.

Some people try
to turn back their
odometers.
Not me,
I want people
to know why I look
this way.
I've traveled
a long way
and some of the
roads weren't
paved.

– Will Rogers

Children today
are tyrants.
They contradict
their parents,
gobble their food
and tyrannize
their teachers.

– Socrates
(Stated approximately
in the year 400 B.C.)

"Exercise is
a dirty word.
Every time I hear it,
I wash my
mouth out
with chocolate."

11

# Today

God, let today not be a time of loss,
but of gain in laughter and understanding…
Let today not be a time of regret,
but of increase in forgiveness and grace…

God, let today not be a time of sorrow, but of acceptance and compassion... Let today not be a time of sadness, but of peace, serenity, and joy.

"My kids got me a cell so I wouldn't have to get up to answer the phone.

Now all I have to do is find it!"

"Ahhh...
it's pure bliss
to do nothing,
and then
rest afterward."

# Ten Happy Things About Getting Older

10. You know all the answers on "Remember When" trivia night.

9. Your kids actually ask for your advice from time to time.

8. You can enjoy people, because you don't care what they think.

7. You realize all those things you used to worry about really don't matter.

6. You're truly thankful to wake up in the morning.

5. You don't have to update your work skills any longer.

4. You feel no obligation to cram your feet into pointy shoes.

3. You can take the vacant seat in a crowded waiting room without feeling guilty.

2. You can decline any invitation, and they'll understand.

And most important of all…

# #1
# You have something in common with everyone else your age- you're still breathing!

# I'll Never Admit It!

● ● ● ● ● ● ● ● ● ● ● ● ● ●

In years I've reached a certain age,
but in my heart, I'm far from there.
It must be some mistake, this stage
of sagging tummy, thinning hair…

"Not I!" I cry when some kid says,
"Here, let me help you cross the street."
Not I! No matter what she sees,
I'm still in charge of my two feet…

Alright, I'm not so spry and hale,
but I won't let this cause me woe–
Though wrinkles tell a different tale,
I've got get up and go
(as long as I take it really, really slow!)

Even if I knew
certainly the world
would end tomorrow,
I would plant
an apple tree today.
-Martin luther

"Do not wish
to be anything
but what you are,
and try to
be that perfectly.

-St. Francis de Sales

"Some TV shows
are pretty refreshing.
You feel pretty good
after you wake up."

# Sweet Revenge

Pay-back Time: when your
children's kids turn 16.

If you're mad at your
daughter-in-law,
give your grandson
## a drum.

Tell your grandchildren
what Mom and Dad
did at their age.

# What is gray hair

but the crown of experience,
or wrinkles but the glory
of having seen many seasons?

They call it the weakness of age…
but what is it except the loss
of prideful self-sufficiency
and the blessed acceptance
of God's unfailing strength?

# Is It Naptime Yet?

When you're a child,
you nap when your mom
tells you you're tired.

When you're an adult,
you nap when you
get tired…

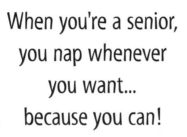

When you're a senior,
you nap whenever
you want...
because you can!

# It's a sure sign your age is showing when...

• • • • • • • • • • • •

- people start telling you how good you look.

- history students start interviewing you for eye-witness reports.

- you're not ticketed for speeding anymore, but pulled over for going too slow.

# Is It Time?

Age doesn't matter.
The best time to think
about retirement is
before the boss does!

"Organic food?
No thanks!
I need all the
preservatives
I can get!"

The novelties
of one generation
are only the
resuscitated
fashions of the
generation
before last.

−George Bernard Shaw

# The Blessings of Years

When you've lived long enough,
  *forgiveness comes readily,*
because you've made
    plenty of blunders yourself…
*fear comes rarely,*
  because frightening events
    are nothing new to you…

When you've lived long enough,
*peace of mind comes naturally,*
because you've found
that few things
are worth fretting over…
and *contentment comes easily,*
because you know
from experience
that the best things in life
are, in fact, free.

An acorn is not an oak
tree when it sprouted.
It must go through
long summers and
fierce winters; it has
to endure all that frost
and snow and winds
can bring before it is
a full grown oak.
So it is with us.

-Henry Ward Beecher

"I've reached the age where I've learned all I'm ever going to learn. The trick is to remember any of it."

Finish each day
and be done with it.
You have done what you could;
some blunders and absurdities
have crept in;
forget them as soon as you can.
Tomorrow is a new day;
you shall begin it serenely
and with too high a spirit
to be encumbered with your
old nonsense.

−Ralph Waldo Emerson

The longer I live,
the more beautiful
life becomes.

-Frank Lloyd Wright

It gives me great
pleasure to converse
with the aged.
They have been over
the road that
all of us travel
and know where it is
rough and difficult
and where it is level
and easy!
- Plato

Far worse than
wrinkled skin is a
wrinkled soul.

-Proverb

# Good Morning!

● ● ● ● ● ● ● ● ● ● ● ● ● ●

It's a good morning for kids when they wake up early and watch cartoons…

It's a good morning for teens when they wake up in the middle of the afternoon…

It's a good morning for adults when they wake up and realize it's Saturday…

It's a good morning for old folks when they wake up.

If wrinkles must be
written upon our brows,
let them not be written
upon the heart.
The spirit should not
grow old.
- James A. Garfield

"Technology
is great-
as long as
I don't have
to use it."

Now that I'm
old enough to know
the answers,
why aren't the young
asking me
any questions?

Youth is the age
to receive instruction,
middle age
to make use of it,
and old age
to impart it to others.
-Pythagoras

May you live
as long as you want,
And never want
as long as you live.

-Irish Blessing

# God's Ways

Coincidence is when God
chooses to remain anonymous.

God has promised a safe landing,
not a calm passage.

If God is your co-pilot,
swap seats-now!

Don't give up on yourself.
God hasn't.

Many folks want to serve God,
but only as advisors.

Seven days without worship
makes one weak.

# Thank God for
## senior moments!

- They clear your mind so you can focus on what's really important (whatever that is).

- They encourage the kids to do things for you that you don't want to do anyway.

- They serve as a good excuse to not recognize people you don't care to talk to…

- They get you off the hook when you forget the name of someone you see every day.

- They give you something to blame when you make a mistake.

- They give the kids something to blame when you embarrass them in public.

## And most of all...

- They remind you that you're a living, breathing, still-functioning human being! (Only with a little mileage on you!)

After looking
through my bills,
I think I can make it
through the rest
of the month
if I don't eat
or turn anything on.

• • • • • • • • • • • •

May you live to be
100 years,
With one extra year
to repent!

−Irish Blessing

• • • • • • • • • • • •

"I love hanging out
with young people.
No matter who
they are,
I know more
than they do!"

"Yep, son, I started
out with nothing...
and I still have
most of it."

# Wisdom

comes from
good judgment,
and a lot of
good judgment
comes from bad
judgment.

–Proverb

"Sure I exercise.
I walk to the
refrigerator and back
to my recliner dozens
of times a day."

At the end of our lives,
we will not be judged
by how many diplomas
we have received,
how much money
we have made, or how
many great things we
have done...

We will be judged by:
I was hungry and you
gave me to eat.
I was naked and
you clothed me.
I was homeless and
you took me in.

−Mother Teresa

Now is no time to
think of what you do
not have. Think of
what you can do with
what there is.

- Ernest Hemingway

If the only prayer
you ever say
in your entire life is
thank you,
it will be enough.

−Meister Eckhart

God grant you
many years to live,
for sure He must
be knowing
That Earth has
angels all too few,
and heaven's
overflowing.

-Irish Blessing

"Isn't it funny how we spent so much time as kids wishing we were older?"

● ● ● ● ● ● ● ● ● ● ● ●

# God bless the people
who bring me joy…
those who show
they care in so many
special ways…

Bless the people
who've given me
cherished memories,
and those who continue
to bring joy to my heart
and a smile to my lips…

Bless the people
whose companionship
I treasure-
and grant that I remain
the kind of person
others are happy
to call "friend."
Amen

● ● ● ● ● ● ● ● ● ● ● ● ●

It is easy to say how
we love new friends,
and what we
think of them,
but words can never
trace out all the
fibers that knit
us to the old.

−George Eliot

# Remembering

People may forget what you said,
and people may forget what you did...
but they'll never ever forget
how you made them feel.

# Shhh!

• • • • • • • • • • • • •

A pious man reached his 100th birthday, and he suddenly stopped going to church. Concerned about his health, his pastor paid him a visit, and was surprised to find the man in exceptionally good shape.

"We've missed you in church lately," the pastor said.

"Oh, I'm not coming anymore," the man replied. "You know, I fully expected the Lord to take me at 90, and then at 95, but He didn't. I think He's forgotten about me, and I certainly don't want to remind Him!"

# Senility Prayer

God grant me the
senility to forget the people
I never liked…

the good fortune
to run into the ones I do…

and the eyesight
to tell the difference.

"Now that I've
finally got my head
on straight,
my body's
falling apart!"

If I'd known
how long I'd live,
I'd have taken
better care
of myself.

"If God wanted me
to touch my toes,
He would have
put them around
my waist!"

# Daily Delivery

• • • • • • • • • • • • • •

"Where's my Sunday newspaper?"
the elderly woman shrieked
into the phone.

"Ma'am," the customer service
agent replied. "It will be delivered
tomorrow. Today is Saturday."

"Oh," the woman said,
feeling sheepish.
"I guess that's why
I was the only one
in church this morning."

An antique is something your grandparents bought for 50¢, your parents sold for $5, and you found at a flea market yesterday for $50.

"OK, so growing
old happens,
but growing up
doesn't have to!"

# You know you're old when...

- you're wearing alligator shoes and a turtle neck, and you're not even dressed yet.

- you've driven the last 20 miles with your right turn signal on.

- you need a permit to light the candles on your birthday cake.

- you take twice as long to look half as good as you used to.

- your idea of weight lifting is getting out of the chair.

- you can't recall having any senior moments!

# Been to the Clinic Lately?

● ● ● ● ● ● ● ● ● ● ● ● ● ●

I've been in this waiting room
so long that I think I've recovered.

I asked my doctor for a second opinion,
so he billed me twice.

I had walking pneumonia,
and my doctor charged me by the mile.

I knew I was in trouble when the doctor
put on his best graveside manner.

"I personally don't mind getting older, but my body's taking it very, very badly."

I know God will not
give me anything
I can't handle.
I just wish that
He didn't trust me
so much.

–Mother Teresa

Let your old age
be childlike,
and your childhood
like old age; that is,
so that neither may
your wisdom
be with pride,
nor your humility
without wisdom.

- Augustine

# Mangled Maxims

• • • • • • • • • • • • • •

Spend each day as if it were your last…
and you'll be broke by sunset.

A journey of a thousand miles begins with…
four words: I know a shortcut.

It doesn't matter whether you win or lose…
until you lose.

You can't take it with you…
or hearses would have luggage
compartments.

There's no fool like an old fool…
though teenagers can offer
some pretty stiff competition.

Things improve with age…
except at class reunions.

● ● ● ● ● ● ● ● ● ● ● ● ● ● ●

# Instructions

Pharmacist to patient:
"Take one of these
every three hours,
or as often as
you can get the cap off."

# Exercise

Sure I run…
to the cookie plate…
to the hot fudge sundae…
to the chili dip…

My doctor told me that
exercise would add years to my life.
He was right.
I feel ten years older already!

"The only way to keep your health
is to eat what you don't want,
drink what you don't like
and do what you'd rather not."
-Mark Twain

# Old age is when...

…women stop worrying
about getting pregnant,
and men start worrying
they look pregnant.

…given a choice between
two invitations, you choose
the one that gets
you home earlier.

…people refer to you as
young-looking instead of young.

…you've stopped growing vertically,
but not horizontally.

# No Sports for Me

• • • • • • • • • • • •

Doctor:
Do you participate in sports?

Senior:
No, my parents won't let me.

Doc:
Your parents?

Senior:
That's right-Mother Nature
and Father Time.

"Life was simpler before credit cards. I didn't have to wait until the end of the month to find out how poor I am."

# Men
# and
# Women

Women always worry
about the things that men
forget; men always worry
about the things
that women remember.

# Faith, Hope, Love

• • • • • • • • • • • • • •

Dear Lord, please bless these years
And keep Your Spirit near
through every day…

Let memories bring me smiles,
And may my present trials
increase my faith…

When aches and pains assail,
let patience never fail
to help me cope…

And when the shadows fall,
Let joy and laughter call
with fervent hope…

Lord, bless this sacred time,
And light these years of mine
from heaven above…

Let gentleness increase,
And fill my soul with peace
and caring love.

• • • • • • • • • • • • • •

I don't need to watch
TV game shows.
If I want to watch
someone make
a lot of money,
I'll just call the
plumber.

They say that age
is all in your mind.
The trick is keeping it
from creeping down
into your body!

"Progress
may have been
all right once,
but in my opinion,
it's gone on
far too long!"

# True Words

• • • • • • • • •

Blessed is the man who,
having nothing to say,
abstains from giving us
wordy  evidence of the fact.
-George Eliot

The difference between
the right word and the
almost right word
is the difference between
lightning and a lightning bug.
-Mark Twain

"Talk is cheap
because supply
exceeds demand."

Take one step
at a time.
At our age,
it's not a choice-
it's a necessity.

I will never be
an old man.
To me, old age
is always fifteen
years older
than I am.

- Bernard Baruch

# At This Age

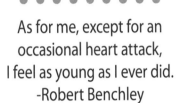

As for me, except for an
occasional heart attack,
I feel as young as I ever did.
-Robert Benchley

Even though we don't have
everything we want,
we can be thankful we don't get
everything we deserve.

Everyone is the age
of his heart.
-Proverb

"I'm getting so
absent minded
that I'm talking,
and in the middle
of a sentence
I just..."

# Life Today

Change is inevitable,
except from a
vending machine.

Problems today
are so complex that even
teenagers don't
have the answers.

If you're not confused,
you don't know
what's going on!

# Let Them Eat Cake

• • • • • • • • • • • • • •

At his last birthday,
the candles cost more
than the cake!

His birthday cake
was condemned
as a fire hazard.

Birthdays are wonderful–
after all,
the more of them you have,
the longer you get to live!

# Looking Good?

Cosmetics:
products used by teens
to feel older, and by seniors
to feel younger.

Toupee:
hairpiece guaranteed to make
you look at least 10 years sillier.

Favorite shirt:
garment that has been
in and out of fashion
at least five times
since it was new.

# Relax!

• • • • • • • • • • • •

After the elderly couple arrived at the lake for a weekend away, the wife exclaimed, "Oh, honey! We have to go back home right away! I'm afraid I left the iron on and it's going to start a fire!"

"Don't worry about it, dear," the husband replied, "I just remembered I left the water running in the kitchen sink."

# Let's Face It!

My eyesight has gotten so bad that I need glasses to see my glasses.

He says he can't believe his ears. Neither can I.

It's funny how when you get older your hair doesn't grow the way it used to...
or in the same places.

I know she has all her own teeth. I was with her when she bought them.

I'm not bald – I'm just too tall for my hair!

Stranger:
Haven't I seen your face someplace else?
Senior:
Nope, it's always been right here between my ears.

Isn't it funny
how those
irritating things
your kids did
seem so adorable
when your
grandchildren
do them?

"If you don't like the way I drive, why don't you get off the sidewalk?"

• • • • • • • • • • •

A good memory
can remember
the day's blessings
and forget
the day's troubles.

• • • • • • • • • • •

"I got out of my
memory-improvement
class, and forgot
where I parked
my car!"

# True Blessings

May God grant you always
a sunbeam to warm you,
a moonbeam to charm you,
a sheltering angel
so nothing can harm you.

Laughter to cheer you,
faithful friends near you,
and whenever you pray,
heaven to hear you.

"Show me a man
who walks with his
head held high,
and I'll show you
a man who hasn't
gotten used to
his bifocals."

# The older you get, you discover that...

● ● ● ● ● ● ● ● ● ● ● ●

- failure isn't permanent

- worry isn't worth it

- there's humor in almost everything

- each morning you wake up
  is a good morning

- time is more precious than you
  ever thought...

- you've survived some mighty hard times

- gratitude is essential

- other people's opinions don't define you

- money isn't everything... really.

● ● ● ● ● ● ● ● ● ● ● ● ●

# Chow Down!

Eat what you like
and let the food
fight it out inside.

–Mark Twain

"I'm not 75!
I'm 35,
with a good 40 years'
experience
behind me!"

# Sunday Snooze

"Crank up the air conditioning, Pastor!"
the elderly man exclaimed.
"It's unhealthy for people to sleep
in a stuffy room!"

# He's so old...

...He knew the first of the Mohicans.

... He orders three-minute eggs
in a restaurant, and they make
him pay in advance.

... He gets winded playing chess.

... He never buys green bananas.

I've been
taught to
respect my elders,
although these
days it's getting
harder and harder
to find them.

# Promises, Promises!

• • • • • • • • • • • •

It was a preacher's last Sunday before he would leave for another church, and one of his elderly parishioners was beside herself with grief. "Now, now," the pastor said, trying to console her. "The next pastor will no doubt be much better."

Through her tears, the woman replied, "But that's what they promised last time!"

I intend
to live forever.

So far, so good.

Once you can accept
the universe as
matter expanding
into nothing that
is something,
wearing stripes with
plaid comes easy.

-Albert Einstein

# Finances

I invested half my money
in paper towels and the other
half in revolving doors.
I was wiped out before
I could turn around!

I have enough money to last me
for the rest of my life if I don't
need to buy anything.

The only way I'll have folding
money in my pocket is if they
put hinges on nickels.

"Last year, it was my doctor who put me on a diet. This year, it was my accountant."

October:
This is one of the peculiarly dangerous months to speculate in stocks.
The others are July, January, September, April, November, May, March, June, December, August, and February.

# It's a pity when...

- store clerks start calling you sweetie.

- you smile so people will mistake your wrinkles for laugh lines.

- instead of learning something new, you start forgetting what you learned.

- you sink your teeth into a good steak, and there they stay.

Have courage
for the great
sorrows of life
and patience for
the small ones;
and when you
have laboriously
accomplished your
daily task,
go to sleep in peace.
God is awake.

–Victor Hugo

# People

There comes a point
in your life when
you realize who
really matters,
who never did…
and who always will.

Drag your
thoughts away
from your troubles...
by the ears,
by the heels,
or any other way
you can manage it.

–Mark Twain

"I got into
the bathtub
this morning
without taking
my clothes off...
which is OK,
because I forgot to
turn on the water."

Aging is kind of
like a cute puppy-
it's a little hairy but
you might as well
embrace it.

# Cruuunch!

I pulled in a parking lot last night,
and it was full of compact cars.
Though they weren't like that before
I arrived.

A senior citizen parked her car on
a slope and it rolled away, crashing into
several vehicles. The officer at the scene
asked her, "Ma'am, why didn't you use
your emergency brake?" Annoyed,
the woman replied, "Since when,
young man, did going to the grocery
store become an emergency?"

A great musician can bring tears to
your eyes. So can an auto mechanic.

Be not afraid of
growing slowly,
be afraid only
of standing still.

- Ancient Proverb

# Bulletin Bloopers

• • • • • • • • • • • • • • • • • •

Remember in prayer
the many who are sick of our
church and community.

The Senior Choir invites any
member of the congregation
who enjoys sinning
to join the choir.

A new loudspeaker system has
been installed in our church.
It was given by one of our
members in honor of his wife.

A bean supper will be held
on Thursday evening.
Music will follow.

Barbara remains in the
hospital and requests your
continued prayers.
She is also having trouble
sleeping and requests tapes
of Pastor Jack's sermons.

● ● ● ● ● ● ● ● ● ● ● ● ● ● ● ● ●

# Thank You, Lord!

● ● ● ● ● ● ● ● ● ● ● ● ● ● ● ● ●

An elderly woman greeted each morning
by opening her window and proclaiming,
"God is good! Praise God for another day!"
Her neighbor, an atheist, was annoyed by her
witness, and he would shout back,
"There is no God!"

One particular morning, the woman realized
she had no money for the day's groceries.
She opened her window and said,
"God is good! Praise God for another day!
And Lord, could You please provide
me with food for today?"

The atheist saw a chance to make his point. He went to the store, bought a bag of groceries, and set them on the woman's porch.

When the woman opened her front door, she exclaimed, "Thank You, Lord, thank You!"

The atheist yelled back gleefully, "Ha, ha! God didn't buy those groceries-I did!"

"Oh Lord, You are awesome!" the woman replied. "You not only brought food to my house, but you got the devil to pay for it!"

● ● ● ● ● ● ● ● ● ● ● ● ● ● ● ● ● ●

# Timeless Truths

It's the great mystery of
human life that old grief passes
gradually into quiet tender joy.
-Fyodor Dostoevsky

The best thing one can do
when it's raining is to let it rain.
-Henry Wadsworth Longfellow

Whatever tears one may shed,
in the end one always
blows one's nose.
-Heinrich Heine

# Weighty Issues

I'm on a strict diet.
I never eat between snacks.

The only exercise he gets is
jumping to conclusions.

The advantage of exercising
every day is that
you'll die healthier.

He certainly watches his weight.
It's right there in front,
where he can keep an eye on it.

"I put my
shoes on the
wrong feet...
but I can't
remember
whose feet
I put them on."

Postcard from
vacationing senior:

"Wish you
were here.
By the way,
where am I?"

# Medical Matters

● ● ● ● ● ● ● ● ● ●

Four out of five doctors
recommend another doctor.

A fool and his money are soon
parted. However, if you go to
a doctor, it will be surgically
removed.

A robber broke into a medical
clinic, and the doctor on duty
charged him for an office visit.

One hospital installed a sand trap in surgery so the doctors can operate in familiar surroundings.

Think how much higher medical costs would be if physicians bought current magazines to put in their waiting room.

The latest miracle drug is so powerful, you have to be in perfect health to start taking it.

● ● ● ● ● ● ● ● ● ● ●

● ● ● ● ● ● ● ● ● ● ●

No wise man
ever wished
to be younger.

- Jonathan Swift

● ● ● ● ● ● ● ● ● ● ●

The belief that youth
is the happiest time
of life is founded
upon a fallacy.
The happiest person
is the person who
thinks the most
interesting thoughts,
and we grow happier
as we grow older.

–William Lyon Phelps

# Remember When...

● ● ● ● ● ● ● ● ● ● ● ● ●

- Bacon, eggs, milk, and sunshine were good for you?

- You chose your cereal for the toy, not for the fiber content?

- Your car's high beam light switch was next to the clutch?

# Zzzz!

Doc:
Do you sleep
soundly?

Senior:
Yep! You should
hear me—
my neighbors do!

# Thank God for age...

● ● ● ● ● ● ● ● ● ● ● ● ● ●

The doubts of youth lie far behind me,
and the anxieties that plagued me
for so long
are gone.

The regrets of yesterday
and fears for tomorrow
have vanished,
replaced by simple pleasure
for today.

Thank God for the day at hand,
for things as they are,
for this season in life...
For in age I have found peace
and heart-deep comfort
in You.

# Amen

● ● ● ● ● ● ● ● ● ● ● ● ●

Many blessings
do the advancing
years bring
with them.
- Horace